ASCD | arias

ENGAGING & CHALLENGING GIFTED STUDENTS

Tips for Supporting Extraordinary Minds in Your Classroom

Jenny Grant **RANKIN**

ASCD

Alexandria, VA USA

Website: www.ascd.org   www.ascdarias.org
E-mail: books@ascd.org

Printed in the United States of America. ASCD publications present a variety of viewpoints. The views expressed or implied in this book should not be interpreted as official positions of the Association.

PAPERBACK ISBN: 978-1-4166-2334-2   ASCD product #SF117019

Also available as an e-book (see Books in Print for the ISBNs).

Library of Congress Cataloging-in-Publication Data

Names: Rankin, Jenny Grant, author.
Title: Engaging & challenging gifted students : tips for supporting
    extraordinary minds in your classroom / Jenny Grant Rankin.
Description: Alexandria, Virginia : ASCD, [2017] | Includes bibliographical
    references.
Identifiers: LCCN 2016034661 (print) | LCCN 2016037682 (ebook) | ISBN
    9781416623342 (pbk.) | ISBN 9781416623366 (PDF)
Subjects: LCSH: Gifted children--Education. | Teachers of gifted children.
Classification: LCC LC3993 .R36 2017 (print) | LCC LC3993 (ebook) | DDC
    371.95--dc23
LC record available at https://lccn.loc.gov/2016034661

24 23 22 21 20 19 18 17   1 2 3 4 5 6 7 8 9 10

ASCD | arias

ENGAGING & CHALLENGING GIFTED STUDENTS

*Tips for Supporting
Extraordinary Minds
in Your Classroom*

Want to earn a free ASCD Arias e-book?
Your opinion counts! Please take 2–3 minutes to give
us your feedback on this publication. All survey
respondents will be entered into a drawing to
win an ASCD Arias e-book.

Please visit
www.ascd.org/ariasfeedback

Thank you!

*This book is dedicated to
my little Piper and her superpower spirit.*

Introduction

Three million to five million students (6 to 10 percent) can be characterized as gifted and talented in the United States (National Association for Gifted Children, 2016). Each gifted child (GC) is unique, and teachers often struggle to both understand and meet the needs of each GC while juggling the needs of non-gifted students.

In this book, GCs constitute those who fit the following description, as provided in a position statement by the National Association for Gifted Children (NAGC) (2011):

> Gifted individuals are those who demonstrate outstanding levels of aptitude (defined as an exceptional ability to reason and learn) or competence (documented performance or achievement in top 10% or rarer) in one or more domains. Domains include any structured area of activity with its own symbol system (e.g., mathematics, music, language) and/or set of sensorimotor skills (e.g., painting, dance, sports). (p. 1)

This book succintly and comprehensively gives you the information you need to identify and meet the needs of each GC. It gives you the "meat" of what you need to avoid common pitfalls and offer each GC the best education possible. This includes recognizing both the signs of disability that many gifted students (known as twice-exceptional) experience and each GC's unique blend of innate intensities (or overexcitabilities) while knowing how best to work with these.

You can implement this book's strategies and tips in your classroom to ensure that each GC is engaged (and not simply compliant) and appropriately challenged. The resources provided at the end of the book will be useful in acquiring help from outside of the classroom.

This book, though focused on GCs, is not meant to imply that non-gifted children (non-GCs) should receive less attention in the classroom. In fact, if you see a strategy in this book that will work well with your non-GCs, by all means use it. In addition, by presenting ways in which you can appeal to the characteristics and interests of GCs, this book is not meant to imply that you should coddle GCs. All strategies should be selected and applied as appropriate for each individual GC to ensure that she will flourish academically, maintain a love of learning, and be armed with the skills necessary to find success and happiness in life.

Identify Gifted Students

Knowing which of your students are gifted is not as easy as it might sound, and some GCs can slip under most teachers' radar. For example:

- **Female and English learners (ELs)**. Both are disproportionately overlooked in referrals for gifted services (Card & Giuliano, 2015).
- **African American and Hispanic students**. These students are significantly less likely than white students to receive gifted services, particularly when they have white teachers. Black students are half as likely as white students to be labeled gifted, even when their test scores are comparable (Grissom & Redding, 2016).
- **Socioeconomically disadvantaged students**. These students typically have less exposure to resources that can help them develop their talents, which can make their giftedness less obvious. Poor students are underrepresented in gifted programs even more than are African American and Hispanic students (Callahan, Moon, & Oh, 2014).
- **Poor-performing students**. GCs often perform poorly in school—and in life. For example, at least 5 percent of GCs fail or drop out of school (Renzulli & Park, 2002), and only 2.86 percent of the 210 highly gifted children in a 35-year study grew up to be highly successful adults (Freeman, 2010).

Thus, giftedness is not always obvious. In addition, as noted by NAGC Director of Public Education Jane Clarenbach, JD:

Large percentages of students are in districts with no Gifted and Talented program, so they are never formally identified. In these cases, teachers are on their own to spot the high ability and support it.

This section features key ways you can identify all GCs in your classroom.

Review Gifted Status

Most school districts use computerized data systems to house student data such as gifted and talented (GT), Gifted and Talented Education (GATE), or Talented and Gifted (TAG) status. Teachers generally have access to these systems, or to the demographic reports that communicate important student data. If your school does not provide you with an account of which of your students have GT/GATE/TAG status, request a list of such students from your administrators.

Encourage your administrators to disaggregate GT/GATE/TAG enrollment data by subgroup to ensure no race, ethnicity, gender, or other subgroup (e.g., EL or socioeconomically disadvantaged) is underrepresented (e.g., if 60 percent of a school's students are American Indian, then approximately 60 percent of the school's GT/GATE/TAG students should be American Indian). If school GT/GATE/TAG data are not regularly assessed for fair inclusion, worthy GCs can slip through the cracks and miss access to advanced learning opportunities.

Push for Universal Screening

Universal screening involves testing all students for giftedness instead of testing only some students based on the recommendations of teachers or parents. Research has shown that universal screening results in increased identification of minority, poor, female, and EL students for gifted programs without the standards for identification being lowered or altered in any way (Card & Giuliano, 2015). Universal screening also helps capture GCs who don't exhibit obvious gifted behavior in the classroom.

Personal Account: Roberto[1], a biracial (African American and Hispanic) student, struggled to sit still and focus in my class. He resisted doing schoolwork for the first few weeks but eventually flourished in my classroom. I had to argue for him to be tested for GATE because his other core subject teachers did not endorse him, and he was failing most of his classes. He also fit the profile of traditionally under-tested students. When Roberto was finally assessed, he passed our district GATE test with ease. This put him on other educators' radar as a student with special gifts that needed to be tapped. If universal screening had been in place in our district, the "close call" of Roberto's potential being overlooked would have been avoided.

You can push for universal screening by sharing the information in this section with administrators. In addition, you can nominate all of your students for gifted testing, regardless of your school's screening policies.

---

[1] The names of the author's students have been changed to respect their privacy.

Push for Comprehensive Assessment

Pushing for a range of assessments helps to capture all GCs, as some giftedness will not necessarily show on all gifted assessments. This is particularly true of poor GCs, who have had reduced chances to develop their aptitudes, and of "2E" (twice-exceptional) GCs with learning disabilities like dyslexia.

In addition, push for assessments that are "culture fair" with reduced bias. For example, the Naglieri Nonverbal Ability Test (NNAT) can identify gifted and talented K–4 students regardless of language or cultural barriers, which can otherwise skew gifted students' test scores. While many schools use homegrown or long-used assessments to identify students for GT/GATE/TAG, it's hard to defend such assessments when the NNAT has had norms set based on more than 10,000 students. Work with administrators to ensure that your school's assessment plan is up to par.

Recognize Intensities for What They Are

As giftedness experts Susan Winebrenner and Dina Brulles (2012) write:

Today, overexcitability, or OE, is considered a marker of giftedness, one of the many things to look for when identifying a gifted child. (p. 11)

Overexcitabilities (OEs) can help teachers spot a GC (Winebrenner & Brulles, 2012). Each GC is likely to have at least one OE that is often misunderstood and sometimes problematic. As these intensities are far less common with non-GCs, teachers are advised to pay heightened attention to spotting OEs in each GC. In other words, non-GCs can sometimes have OEs, whereas GCs nearly always have OEs, even if an intensity is masked and thus unlikely to be spotted. Most GCs have two to five innate intensities, though they vary in dominance and one type usually stands out as the most dominant. Kazimierz Dabrowski (1902–1980) characterized these OEs in a manner still used today: emotional, imaginational, intellectual, psychomotor, and sensual.

Each of the Five OEs

Explanations of these OEs, as well as strategies for working with a GC with a given OE, can be found at http://www.ascd.org/ASCD/pdf/books/rankin2016.pdf (or click on "Online Bonus Content" on the book's Table of Contents on the ASCD website—http://www.ascd.org/publications/books/sf117019.aspx). (Note: A GC need not display every characteristic associated with an OE in order to have the OE.)

For All Types of Intensities

For all OEs, be on the lookout for chances to commend and celebrate the intensities when their impact is positive.

For instance, if a science-obsessed GC is able to list all the elements on the periodic table, let her perform this feat for the class (before a related lesson) and afterward initiate a loud applause.

Also, set appropriate boundaries that will prevent the GC from disrupting his or his classmates' learning. For example, if I taught a GC with the psychomotor OE who often blurted out in class, I might:

- Set aside time to speak with the GC and his parent(s) about the matter and gather feedback on what triggers the behavior and what works best to discourage the behavior. Note that both the parent and GC can be invaluable sources for this information. Other teachers and support staff can offer additional input.
- Identify and nurture the GC's unique gifts. Colucci (2015), an award-winning teacher, describes one of his GCs who talked incessantly. When Colucci realized speaking was the child's strongest gift, rather than fight it, he channeled it into literature circles, presentations, vocabulary activities, and collaborative work.
- Establish a reward system as necessary. For example, I might say to the GC "Whenever you make it through the whole discussion without blurting out, I'll call on you as the last student to share your thoughts on the lesson." Note this is not a material reward. GCs are usually unmotivated by token rewards like candy or toys, whereas they are motivated by rewards that engage their natural interests and needs.

- Establish consequences as necessary. For example, I might say to the GC "If you blurt out during the discussion once, I won't call on you; if you blurt out more than once, you won't get to be the line leader, as leaders need to respect others' turns." Whatever the consequence, make it something that matters to the child, something related to the disturbance, and something paired with a "check in" talk. The consequence should not be one that isolates, demeans, or exacerbates the OE with which the GC is struggling.

  Personal Account: When I was a long-term 3rd grade substitute teacher, as another student led the post-discussion line across campus, I would walk with the GC. I checked on how she was feeling, ensured that she understood why she lost the privilege of being the leader of the line, and discussed what triggered the disruption and what she could do differently if she was again faced with the same trigger. I made sure to do this constructively and in a way that let her know I was trying to help her, while stressing that mistakes are normal and trying is what matters most.

If the OE is distracting or obvious to the GC's peers, view this as a chance to celebrate diversity. If students ask why a GC with the psychomotor OE plays with chair bands with his feet, explain that some people think better when they move. Point out that the GC's high energy might make him better at sports and staying healthy, or allow him to spread enthusiasm or accomplish more than the average person. Explain that all people are different and that our uniqueness helps make us interesting and able to offer different gifts to the world. Point out other students' unique, beneficial qualities, and celebrate the diversity of your classroom (always being sensitive to which students might feel uncomfortable being singled out).

Personal Account: I had a GC named Henry, whose psychomotor OE left him ever-ready to vacate his seat, whom I often asked to pass out things like papers or supplies to the class. Henry's peers took notice of the pattern and started calling him "Helpful Henry" as he was always ready to help with these tasks. While some students would have felt teased by the playful barb, Henry, who loved to joke around, grinned at the name and hammed it up for the crowd. For example, he'd bow to me upon accepting a stack of papers and say, "Happy to help, m'lady!" I'd respond, "Wow, I love how helpful Henry is!" or "We're so lucky Henry is helpful, or you'd never get your papers back!" Students would laugh, but they'd also see and hear about how this energetic GC's "being different" added joy to and benefited the class.

On occasion, GCs can qualify for Individualized Education Programs (IEPs) and Behavior Intervention Plans (BIPs). Before considering these options (which should only be used in extreme cases), employ strategies for working with GCs that are within your control as a teacher, as those strategies might be all that are needed to help GCs with OEs succeed in your classroom.

Engage Each Child

As with other students, a GC's compliance in the classroom and with homework does not automatically equate to true engagement. A lack of engagement can result when a GC is not sufficiently challenged by classwork, but the issue of rigor will be addressed in the next section. This section covers assorted strategies readers can implement to make GCs excited to participate and learn within the context of the classroom.

When struggling or off-task students overtake a teacher's time, as often occurs, GCs are robbed of the teacher's attention. Thus, keeping non-GCs engaged is an important part of being "freed up" to give GCs the equivalent attention they deserve. We want GCs engaged in an inclusive classroom, and many of this section's strategies also work well with non-GCs.

Differentiation

Key to effective learning for all students is adjusting instruction to appeal to students' individual needs. Differentiation can involve making adjustments to allow for varied learning levels (covered in the next section), or to allow for varied learning preferences such as preferred learning style, topics of interest, and the like (covered in this section). Matching learning tasks to a GC's preferences enhances her engagement and motivation to learn, while bolstering feelings about school (Rogers, 2002; Stanley, 2012). Since a GC's unique qualities and preferences can be particularly intense, differentiation is especially vital to their engagement. When determining variations, keep the interests and characteristics of individual GCs in mind so you can offer alternatives that mesh well with these, and so you can point out possibilities to students.

Differentiation can require adjustments to your instruction so students can work on different things while still harmonizing within the same classroom. Explore stations, cooperative learning, project-based learning (PBL), interactive technology (for which your school and district technology leaders can give you guidance and tools), and additional options that allow you to vary learning opportunities while circulating among students. For example, PBL allows GCs to set their own paces and structure their own tasks while learning alongside non-GCs in the classroom (Stanley, 2012). Since it is common for GCs to outpace their non-GC peers within their gifted areas, options that allow multiple paces to operate within the same classroom (like PBL or student-centered technologies) are especially vital. The same goes for options that allow multiple roles to operate within the same classroom (like cooperative learning or stations), given GCs' common superiority in ability. Likewise, GCs' common intensity in interests is another reason that differentiated options allowing GCs to follow those interests are especially vital for GCs. Volunteers (such as parents and retired teachers) can help manage groups who have differentiated tasks within the classroom.

Collaboration, which will be discussed in detail, will make the task of differentiating manageable. Here are some more specific ways of using differentiation to make a positive difference for your GCs:

- Let students choose from learning options in the classroom. For example, set up stations for different tasks (all appropriate for the same lesson unit, but with options that introduce complexity and rigor specific to your GC) and allow students to work at the station that most interests them, or provide supplies for all options and students can work where they are on any choice that interests them. When you allow all students in a class to select from different tasks to learn the same concept in different ways, class discussions at the end about what students learned are enhanced by their varied experiences and exposure to different sources (Winebrenner, 2001).

  Personal Account: While teaching English for a high school's summer school program, I had a GC named Vicky who, because she was not motivated to earn a passing grade during the school year, now had to make up the credits. My other students had reading and writing skills far below grade level, so there was an ability chasm between Vicky and the rest of the class. I used a variety of differentiations with Vicky, as described in this section of the book, and providing options was an approach that worked especially well. For example, on a lesson about tone, I let students choose between three short stories by American authors (the focus of the class). Students could then choose a synthesized means of demonstrating their understanding of the story's tone, which they could either turn in or present to the class so we could discuss different interpretations. Students could produce a short story, song, or rap that communicated the same tone as the story (most students chose the rap option), or they could write an essay supporting their claims about the story's tone or comparing/contrasting its tone to that of one of the other two stories. I added "bonus challenge" suggestions for each option as well. I arranged supply stations around the room so students would have access to essay graphic organizers, templates, tone reference sheets, and the like.

As early as the second day of class, it was clear Vicky was highly engaged. She was naturally quiet, but she would pay close attention, push herself, and produce polished work. I often gave Vicky the freedom to pursue an option of her own design, and she did so responsibly (challenging herself). Thus, for the tone project, which I assigned near the end of summer school, I expected Vicky to do the same and was surprised when she chose to write a rap like the other students. But Vicky had a bigger surprise in store for me. Shy Vicky, upon the urging of her peers, agreed to perform her rap for the class. She never looked up from her page, but she rocked the room with her words. Instead of communicating the tone of Poe's *The Tell-Tale Heart* while also rapping about what happened in the story, as other students had done, Vicky rapped about a young woman who cheated on her boyfriend with a short kiss and hid the new man's love note in her locker. The way Vicky wove Poe's story's tone into her rap, while also using Poe's literary tactics like repetition, was nothing less than stunning. When this shy GC finished, the praise that rained down on her from all over the classroom must have been a shining moment in Vicky's life. All because this special GC was given differentiated options and was engaged to rise to the occasion.

- Just as in class assignments, let students choose from options within homework assignments. List a variety of ways in which students may complete an assignment (or a portion of an assignment) that include more rigorous options that would most appeal to the interests of your GCs, allowing students to pick the option they like best.

- Let students choose from activities in the classroom that appeal to a variety of GC characteristics. For example, allow students to choose to work in pairs, in groups, or alone. Some options might involve physical activity, appealing to psychomotor GCs (e.g., "measure your jumps under varied conditions, like when using the plank or carrying the resistance pack, to test your hypotheses) while other options might appeal to more meditative students.

- Let GCs choose the product by which they will demonstrate they have mastered a particular lesson. Stanley (2012) recommended PBL choices such as a demonstration, essay/research paper, exhibition, multiple-choice test (for which the GC provides a detailed rationale for right answers), performance, portfolio, and presentation. He described a student who turned the performance option into an online video game he developed in which a knight's quest taught viewers about physical and chemical changes.

- Let GCs get creative with lesson instructions, as long as they stay true to the spirit of assignments. For example, if a GC wants to build a solar-powered robotic insect instead of completing a worksheet on how solar power works, encourage her to do so. Other GCs might complete most of the assignment but skip steps along the way; this is fine as long as mastery of the concept is achieved. For example, many GCs resist writing because it can actually slow down their thinking and is frequently not necessary as they master a concept (Winebrenner, 2001). Thus, a GC might be allowed to skip journaling his thoughts during the course of a project.

- Offer suggestions for ways individual GCs can veer from lesson instructions to incorporate particular interests. You can make these suggestions verbally or, if easier, give the student a printed or e-mailed message about the option when it's on your mind. For example, a message to a GC obsessed with superheroes might read, "On tomorrow's assignment, feel free to write about how each founding father's position in the debate reminds you of a particular superhero (instead of the assignment's instructions to draw comparisons to people you know)."

- Long (2013) of the National Education Association shares one way to differentiate is to ask GCs to find their own examples of a concept and to explain it to the rest of the class. This also benefits non-GCs, who gain access to lessons taught with peer language.

Personal Account: When I took Model United Nations (UN) in high school, a class with many GCs, our teacher was great at asking GCs to explain concepts in constructive ways. On some days, he'd use previous measures to station us in readiness-based groups. Students who had scored mid-range on a concept would get started on their activity. Meanwhile, those of us who had already mastered the concept would be briefly paired with low performers for our "starter challenge." In these pairs, we GCs would have a (timed) minute each to give "the best explanation possible" of the concept while applying it to our country (in Model UN, each student is assigned a country). The low-performing listeners, who had the task of being the judges, would vote on the explanation they liked best while mirroring how voting occurs in Model UN. This practice helped GCs solidify the concept in our own minds before we moved on to more advanced work for the rest of the class period. This also helped the low performers hear the concept explained in a variety of ways in peer-friendly language, while still requiring them to come up with their own applications to their own countries, preparing them to work on mastering the concept. The system also complemented Model UN structure, kept low-performers in a respected and contributing role, and helped the teacher manage different mastery levels within a single class. The overall experience was positive and *all* students—gifted or not—would greatly benefit from similar activities in classrooms today. The only piece I would change would be to opt for labels that are more positive and pertinent to the role in an activity—such as "judge" or "presenter"—as opposed to his choice of very direct labels based on the previous day's performance—High, Medium, and Low.

Note how this approach differs from asking the GC to teach the lesson or tutor peers—as using a GC as a teacher assistant is detrimental. Also note this would be one of numerous, changing ways a teacher would offer differentiated options to GCs.

- Consider giving a GC less direction on a project. Gently guiding GCs in a general direction, while leaving it up to GCs to choose the path by which they will each achieve the final outcome, gives GCs more freedom to learn (Stanley, 2012).

- Break "rules" as appropriate. For example, you might require students to keep their eyes on you while you speak, but a particular GC with the sensual OE might have trouble remaining attentive with his head up for so long. In that case, you could make an exception to the eye contact rule provided you could verify the student still listened effectively (e.g., follows your directives, notes reflect what is said, and/or he doesn't lapse into a glazed, daydreaming look).
- Set up a station where students can complete a more advanced lesson (different each day) any time they have already mastered the day's regular content. This group should be fluid, meaning students can move in and out of it for each new lesson any time their mastery of that lesson varies. This avoids tracking, which involves locking students into a set level they remain in day after day without reassessment of their assignment to that level. Tracking is known to block lower-performing students from their maximum potential and to commonly reflect too low a judgment of minority and socioeconomically disadvantaged students' capabilities.

Figure 1 presents additional examples of ways to differentiate for GCs. Note differentiating instruction is an umbrella term that is involved in every differentiated aspect. For example, as you differentiate the *process* through which GCs engage in a lesson, you are pairing that with the appropriate instruction to support that differentiated process and interacting with the GC in whatever way will best support her.

FIGURE 1: Differentiation Examples

Aspect to Differentiate	Description	Example of Differentiating for a GC
Environment	Where the student engages in the lesson	An easily overstimulated GC might be more likely to complete an activity in a quiet corner during a particularly boisterous group lesson.
Lesson Content (Curriculum)	Learning objective, tools, etc.	If a Harry Potter-obsessed GC is bored coloring the cell structure diagram, ask her to draw the cell structure of a muggle and identify how this might differ from that of a wizard.
Process	How students engage in the lesson, activities they can do, etc.	While students are "dragging and dropping" pre-written words to form sentences in a computer program, a GC might instead write sentences freely within Word or another word processing program.
Product (Assessment for Formative & Summative Purposes)	How students demonstrate progress and mastery of content	If a GC who loves computer programming is disengaged in writing algebraic expressions, let him translate the expressions to code within a programming environment he likes to use.

Collaboration

Differentiation is crucial to engaging GCs. But preparing variations on assignments, including options from which students can choose, takes additional planning time. Fortunately, teachers can strategically reduce this added workload through collaboration. Collaborating with colleagues on lesson planning is key, and can go so far as to give the differentiation-ready teacher less work than she had prior to collaborating. Here are some ways you can collaborate so that creating, securing, or modifying engaging lessons becomes a realistic task:

- When picking collaborators, look for colleagues who share your work ethic, and with whom you get along well.
- Begin any collaboration by establishing a schedule (like when you'll meet and deadlines for completing lessons), norms (like being on time and turning off cell phones for meetings), and goals (like how much you'll complete together).
- Consider picking a single colleague with whom you would like to collaborate. You can start small, with a single lesson you plan together, and figure out what works best for the two of you. You can always add more collaborators once you have established a successful system.
- Establish an effective professional learning community (PLC) devoted to differentiating lessons for all learners. This usually involves colleagues from your school, but can also involve colleagues from other

schools or even an online community or professional learning network (PLN). Administrators can typically help you form a PLC if you share your interest and purpose with them.

The more you collaborate, the better your group gets at co-planning, and the less work there is for everyone. Just be sure PLC members are adept (or become adept) at crafting engaging, GC-appropriate modifications for each lesson. If needed, administrators can typically secure professional development in this area.

Some teachers like to sit down together the whole way through a lesson's creation, whereas other teachers like to divide the work (e.g., "You plan the warm up, examples/modeling, and quiz, and I'll plan the lesson's main activities—all with GC-ready modifications, of course"). As you build differentiation for GCs into each lesson, you might find that coming together for this part of the planning results in more ideas (like more GC-appropriate options) from which GCs can benefit.

- Trade off with a fellow teacher. Many administrators support teachers trading off watching the GCs when they come together for a differentiated activity. For example, you send your GCs to a colleague's classroom for certain accelerated activities the colleague has planned one week, and the next week you return the favor.
- Articulate with higher-grade teachers, as many have ready-made curriculums appropriate for GCs ready to

skip ahead. This is especially helpful when curriculum sets do not provide extension suggestions.

Participation and Peer Relations

Providing GCs with engaging academics goes more smoothly if you help GCs navigate social and emotional classroom dynamics. For example:

- Be wary of common "group work" pitfalls. True cooperative learning involves all students contributing. This model can become harder to achieve when one student in a group is smarter than the rest. Often, the GC receives added pressure from the group to do most of the work, and this can sour her feelings about school (not to mention rob the other students of learning). If you have students work in groups, become well-versed in ways to keep the workload fair. For example, have the work divided equally, with each student responsible for a particular aspect, and grade or assess students individually. In a poster project I assigned my English students to develop plot points, I modeled the project after the game Clue and gave each student his or her own set of tasks to complete on the project through the perspective of whichever game character the student selected. Each student in the group had a set of paper slips in a particular color, which she pasted on the poster. This made it easy for me to assess who contributed what to the poster, and reminded students their work had to carry its own weight.

- Carefully consider pairings. When placing students in groups or partnerships, it usually works best to pre-plan pairings rather than let students pick with whom they will work. Otherwise, GCs might end up with partners hoping to use them, or GCs can end up with partners who don't challenge them to push themselves. Consider those risks to pick pairings that will push all students to contribute their best.

- Leverage data. When pre-planning groups, it helps to use pre-lesson data. For example, at the end of the previous day's class, ask students three multiple-choice questions you can quickly scan and one open-ended question you can quickly assess to get an idea of how well students know the concept with which they will be working. If the questions include some tutorial information, this can double as an added way to ease students into the next day's content. This readiness data, paired with your understanding of students' needs and how they work with one another, can help you shape groups.

  Depending on the activity these groups will tackle, one option is to devote each group to a single level so the work isn't dumped on the highest-performing kid and so GCs will challenge and push each other. Another option is to make each group an even mix of all levels. In this case, it is especially important to give each student a well-delineated role that will be graded or assessed individually.

- Facilitate more involved, liberated GC participation in learning activities. GCs benefit when teachers assume a "guide on the side" approach rather than a "sage on the stage" method (Azzam, 2016). PBL holds great possibilities for providing constructive student freedoms in this way.

  Case in Point: High school students Violet and Kjersti became so successful and invested in a robot-making program for students that they chose to mentor younger students in robotics to ensure the program's survival (Edutopia, 2013). Violet described how school is more engaging and appealing to smart kids when students are asked to solve complex problems, rather than complete typical schoolwork. Kjersti noted how new and hard robotics was, which presented an exciting challenge. They described how the program's projects made them encounter failures, which helped them to problem solve and apply creativity.

- Be sensitive to whether a GC is an introvert or an extrovert. For example, give an introverted GC added assistance with social development and the ability to work alone or take a moment of solitude during grouping exercises, and give an extroverted GC more hands-on experiences within a learning environment (Fonseca, 2011).

- Be sensitive to GCs' reactions and preferences. For example, some GCs will be mortified if you single them out with praise (e.g., "Look at this amazing poster Juan did!") whereas other GCs are largely driven by such affirmations. Adjust your approach for each GC.

Challenge Each Child

Boring GCs with an unchallenging curriculum threatens to kill their lifelong love of learning and hinders their advancement. As Winebrenner and Brulles (2012) point out, you are required to document how students have mastered assigned standards, but this doesn't mean you have to teach standards to students who have already mastered them. Use the following strategies to ensure each GC is challenged at her appropriate level.

Acceleration

Being a GC should never equal more work time, just deeper and more stimulating work. Acceleration, which involves basing curriculum complexity on a GC's readiness, causes GCs to outperform peers on performance assessments, future university status and career achievement, college grades, and more (Colangelo, Assouline, & Gross, 2004). Many acceleration strategies fit in the category of "curriculum compacting," which allows students to skip unnecessary lessons or lesson segments. (See the section on "Differentiation" for tips on how to manage the "added work" of offering accelerated curriculum.) Consider the following:

- Assess students at the onset of learning (e.g., at the start of the year or before you teach a lesson or unit). This way, if GCs have already mastered content you are about to teach, you can spare them the lessons they don't need.

For example, at the end of the previous day, students can have a chance to complete the hardest task(s) from the next day's lesson. This gives the teacher adequate planning time, though some teachers are comfortable letting students jump to the hardest tasks the day of the lesson (having a harder lesson on hand). Students who can already ace the hardest tasks can be directed to a more advanced activity. Eighty percent or 90 percent or more can be considered mastery, adding mastery bonus points as necessary to make this an A if it is added to a gradebook, as an obsession with perfection won't encourage GCs to take risks and try new things (Winebrenner & Brulles, 2012).

The chance to prove mastery should be open and grouping should be flexible (e.g., newly formed each day or for each lesson) to avoid tracking. For example, GC expert Dina Brulles offers the "most difficult first" approach to all students in her class, and students who can do the five hardest problems don't have to complete that night's homework (Azzam, 2016). The number of "most difficult first" items you select for curriculum compacting will depend on what is appropriate for the assignment, and you can even offer students the chance to take a culminating assessment at the start of an entire unit (Winebrenner & Brulles, 2012).

Many response to intervention (RTI) model implementations at schools successfully support assessment that informs follow-up grouping to support needs, offering higher-achieving students (who are often, but not always, GCs) time away from the kind of lessons lower-achieving students require. Use as many approaches to differentiating instruction as are necessary to facilitate acceleration—whatever will give students the help they need without taxing students with help they don't need.

- Use whichever of these acceleration approaches will best serve the GC: speeding up the lesson, skipping to future/harder parts of the lesson, skipping to a higher-grade/level lesson on the same topic, going more in-depth on the same topic, or working on entirely different content.
- For every lesson you teach, have content on hand (prepared in advance) for students ready to accelerate, just as you have support tools ready for struggling students. In terms of speeding up the lesson, this can mean spending less time giving the GC instructions, modeling fewer examples to get him started, shortening the time he has to complete the lesson, and/or simply allowing him to race through at his own accelerated pace. This option should only be selected if the GC will learn something important from the activity. In other words, if the work is easy because

the GC has already mastered the content, don't have her do the easy parts—or the entire task.

As regards skipping to future or harder parts of the lesson or skipping to a higher-grade or higher-level lesson on the same topic, you can find this content in your classroom, school, or district. Keep records of how GCs advance through any next-grade curriculum so you can articulate well with their next year's teachers (otherwise GCs face repetition). Higher-grade teachers are also excellent sources of support, and allowing students to leave your classroom for particular lessons in higher-grade classrooms is an ideal arrangement for many GCs. For going more in-depth on the same topic or working on entirely different content, the first year of securing lesson enhancements can be a strain. However, you can use them for years to come, and collaborating with colleagues can reduce everyone's workload while benefiting GCs schoolwide (see section "Engage Each Child" for more information). Pull-out programs run by other adults (where GCs leave the room during more remedial instruction to tackle advanced concepts elsewhere) can also help GCs while taking the preparation burden off the teacher.

Personal Account: One of my most rewarding experiences as a gifted third grader was being pulled out of class twice per week for a parent-run book club in which the school's GCs were led in high-school-level literary discussions. I assume this cost the school little or nothing in resources, yet it was a time each day when my engagement could come alive. Not every parent has the expertise of a teacher, but some are content experts or former teachers with much to offer.

Again, any performance-based grouping should be fluid so students have access to gifted content anytime they are ready for it.

- When determining curricular adjustments, draw inspiration from the rigor resources shown in Figure 2. These resources will inform how you "up" the rigor of learning tasks. Examples of such adjustments include asking students to evaluate evidence rather than just find it, asking students to investigate a concept across disciplines rather than within a single context, and requiring students to synthesize varied information as a new construct.

The same projects non-GCs are working on can often be enhanced for GCs. Consider how particular learning tasks can be tweaked (in terms of the resources you studied on depth and complexity, and so on) so the GC delves deeper into content and thinking. For example, English class tasks in Figure 3 have been enhanced in ways that allow GCs' instruction to run seamlessly alongside non-GCs' instruction. Though the tasks are planned for GCs, non-GCs should always have the option of completing the harder tasks.

FIGURE 2: **Rigor Resources**

Concept	Sample Resource	Focus for GC
Bloom's Taxonomy	John Kennedy's expansion of Benjamin Bloom's work at https://commons.wikimedia.org/wiki/File:Blooms_rose.svg	The Analysis, Synthesis, and Evaluation Levels[1]
Depth and Complexity	Jere Fitterman's chart on Sandra Kaplan's work at http://sagtgifted.homestead.com/pdf/Depth_and_Complexity_Chart.pdf	All
Depth of Knowledge (DoK)	Oregon Department of Education's chart on Norman Webb's work at www.ode.state.or.us/teachlearn/subjects/socialscience/standards/depthofknowledgechart.pdf	Level of Complexity 3 (Strategic Thinking) and 4 (Extended Thinking)

[1]Some people prefer to switch the order of Synthesis and Evaluation, and Application can be appropriate if the application is complex.

FIGURE 3: **Sample English Class Tasks**

Task Type	Regular Level Task	Enhanced Task
Calling on Students	Students answer questions.	GCs provide evidence and arguments to back up their answers to questions.
Reading	Students read *Aesop's Fables* for a unit on theme.	GCs read *The Canterbury Tales* for a unit on theme.
Writing	Students write about how theme enhances one of *Aesop's Fables*.	GCs compare and/or contrast how theme enhances one of *The Canterbury Tales* compared to how theme enhances one or a variety of *Aesop's Fables*.
Project	Students create posters in which they illustrate events in their life that fit themes from *Aesop's Fables*.	GCs create posters in which they illustrate events in history that fit themes from *The Canterbury Tales*.
Discussion Stations	Students share and discuss answers/ideas.	GCs debate answers with one another, perhaps even until favorite, hybrid solutions are agreed upon.

Be prepared to "up" the content. On any given day, curriculum you have planned for a GC might work well (e.g., keeps her as challenged as other students in the class are with their curriculum), particularly if the content is already accelerated. However, sometimes a GC will find an assignment to be too easy, or may race through it. You'll want to be prepared with challenging content for these instances.

If you set up a streamlined system for this content (e.g., the GC knows he can always find a more advanced lesson at the yellow table), the GC can get started without interruption whenever necessary, and you can find unobtrusive times to check in with the GC. This can be a list of activities from which students can choose, or a "Bonus Box" from which students can draw a surprise activity. Ensure that: the options change often (such as being specific to each assignment, or replaced weekly); the activities are desirable and not perceived as added/unwanted work; and the GC's learning is varied and appropriate for the subject(s) you are teaching. For example, though allowing the GC to pursue her own academic interest in programming works well in some instances, you don't want to let her spend every spare moment programming and none on the subject you teach.

Involvement and Attitude

- Remain involved. While some GCs work well with self-sufficient learning, other GCs are not likely or developmentally ready to complete lessons independently.

Personal Account: When I was in elementary school, I was grade levels above the other students and was told to "do" the junior high school math books while the rest of the class learned grade-level math. Since I loved to draw, I spent this time doodling quietly. No teacher ever checked in on me during this time or followed up on how I was advancing through the books. I thus received no math instruction for years, simply because I was gifted. GCs deserve teacher involvement, just as other students do, to support their progress.

- Promote a relationship where the GC knows you want to know anytime he is not feeling challenged, and that you will react by providing him with more stimulating content. This means having more rigorous content on hand for every lesson, and it can mean swallowing frustration when a GC interrupts your lesson flow.
- Focus on growth mindset in your classroom. This can prevent GCs from resisting or resenting having to do harder work. Growth mindset involves praising effort rather than innate ability and encourages students to push themselves. Conversely, praising right answers and things that come easy to GCs can promote complacency. Sources such as Dweck (2008) can prove helpful.
- Help the GC's parent determine if major acceleration is needed. For example, there are pros and cons to

grade skipping, making this a very individual decision, whereas most GCs benefit from full-time gifted programs. The whole child needs to be considered by everyone in a position to help her, and teachers are in prime position to advocate for appropriate acceleration.

- Provide GCs with opportunities to work with other GCs. Most GCs thrive and push themselves while learning alongside their gifted peers. While this interaction might occur within your classroom, note it could involve pulling GCs from numerous classrooms during a formal (e.g., regularly scheduled) or informal (e.g., GCs master the content and are ready for something deeper) pullout arrangement. Just be wary of scheduling these times during lunch or recess, as GCs shouldn't be robbed of their free time.

  Be prepared for competitiveness, which frequently occurs when GCs work together. You might begin a meeting or activity with a discussion about sportsmanship, or establish group norms such as "don't taunt," "don't monopolize a project," "let all voices be heard," and "congratulate and encourage one another."

Enrichment

Enrichment can describe times when GCs work on a topic with added depth and breadth. Class-assignment-based enrichment was discussed in the sections on engaging each child and acceleration. Following are additional suggestions for enrichment that can involve people and/or resources outside the classroom:

- Reach out to experts in fields related to the content you teach and the interests of your GCs. With parent consent, you can allow a student to interview a scientist or artist via Skype while you lead the class in another lesson, or a retired professor can volunteer in your classroom to work with your GCs.
- Have GCs shape their work for larger audiences. For example, while you help the class plan more standard science experiments, help your GCs perfect their projects as submissions for the local science festival; as you guide the class in speech basics, help your GCs polish their presentations as submissions for TEDxYouth Talks (www.ted.com/participate/ organize-a-local-tedx-event/community-resources/ event-type-resources/youth-event-resources); or while you help the class craft more standard essays, help your GCs shape their work as submissions for Young Mensan Magazine (www.us.mensa. org/read/ym2-young-mensan-magazine) or other youth publications.

Turn to colleagues, parents, and the Internet to discover opportunities like these. Also, teach GCs to dream big: a publication or venue doesn't have to be designed for child submissions for a GC to produce a compelling piece worthy of being highlighted. *Case in Point*: 15-year-old Jack Andraka was reading an article on single-walled carbon nanotubes in his biology class when he thought of the concept behind his award-winning method for early-stage pancreatic cancer detection (BBC, 2012). Rather than keep his discovery to himself, Jack shared his findings through science fairs, TED Talks, radio interviews, his own book, and other notable venues.

- Expose GCs to contests. For example, suggest a GC pick a class project topic that can double as an entry for the Genes in Space Competition (www.genesinspace. org) or Google Science Fair (www.googlesciencefair. com/en); while you help the class craft grade-level presentations, help your GCs create theirs as films for the White House Student Film Festival (www. whitehouse.gov/filmfest); or after a GC masters a math or science concept, help him explain it in an entry for the Breakthrough Junior Challenge (www. breakthroughjuniorchallenge.org), where he could earn a $250,000 scholarship.

  Turn to colleagues, parents, and the Internet to discover opportunities to perfect work for competition. Contests also give GCs opportunities to control competitiveness, with which many GCs (particularly psychomotor GCs) struggle.

- Involve the GC in authentic learning opportunities. Authentic learning involves providing students with a challenge to solve by determining, designing, and producing a product that helps the world in some way.

The Rocket Ready program is one such example. Rocket Ready teachers can build instruction around a world problem requiring a solution (such as harnessing wind power for electricity in ways third world countries can replicate). These solutions can then double as products for authentic assessment, which involves measuring performance via a "real world" task and is argued to be more meaningful than typical (e.g., multiple choice) tests. Authentic learning can be especially meaningful for GCs with the intellectual OE who can be preoccupied with life's big problems.

- Connect the GC with organizations that offer enrichment. For example, Mensa offers local youth programs (www.us.mensa.org/learn/gifted-youth) through which GCs can meet for enriching activities. Also, Johns Hopkins University's Center for Talented Youth (CTY) (http://cty.jhu.edu/talent/index.html), Duke University's Talented Identification Program (Duke TIP) (https://tip.duke.edu), and Northwestern University's Center for Talent Development (CTD) (www.ctd.northwestern.edu) offer programs that nurture GC's personal and intellectual growth.
- Coordinate with the GC's parent(s) to stay abreast of her extracurricular activities so you can find ways to integrate related projects into your classroom. For example, if the GC attends a poetry slam event, you might ask her to reimagine a Shakespearean sonnet as a slam-worthy poem.

- Encourage the GC to participate in extracurricular activities, and ask parents to tell you when they learn of free opportunities, which you can then share with all parents (see the section entitled "Socioeconomically Disadvantaged" for related ideas). *Case in Point*: Colucci (2015) describes a shy student named Aubrey who joined an Odyssey of the Mind (www.odysseyofthemind.com) program. The club gave her a safe place to express her humor and creativity, and this led to her being more open in Colucci's class, which made it easier for her to reach her goals.

Catch Hidden Challenges

Giftedness does not ensure academic success or ease. However, by watching for challenges GCs commonly face, teachers can help GCs overcome them. The information that follows will help you provide GCs with added support appropriate for specific difficulties.

Asynchronous Development

A child's cognitive, physical, and emotional development can occur at different rates. This asynchronous development is common for GCs, whose cognitive development typically outpaces the GC's physical and emotional maturity. For example, a GC in 2nd grade might look his age and grapple with losing his baby teeth and occasional bedwetting, while simultaneously reading works by Chaucer and Dickens, while throwing the occasional tantrum when he doesn't get his way. Problems caused by asynchronous development can be compounded for GCs who skipped grade levels to be in your classroom, as their physical and emotional development is out of sync with that of their peers.

Rubenstein, Schelling, Wilczynski, and Hooks (2015) found asynchronous development presents challenges for students, families, and schools. For example, some GCs have trouble fitting in with non-GCs, and adults used to the GC's mature reasoning can become more frustrated with his emotional outbursts than they would of an average child or one with cognitive impairment. Teachers can help ease such challenges:

- Watch for signs of bullying and interfere early if you see signs of mistreatment. For example, speak with the GC to try to learn the nature and extent of the problem, pair her with a counselor to help her navigate peer dynamics, speak with ringleaders early to head off trouble (e.g., "The other students look to you as a leader, and a good leader looks out for those who are smaller or younger"), and work with district staff who oversee bullying prevention.
- Involve others as necessary. Counselor involvement can alleviate issues such as perfectionism, low self-esteem, identity issues, ability-hiding, or depression/suicide, all of which often plague GCs. Also, work

closely with parents regarding any concerns you have about a GC's emotional struggles.

- Pair the GC with a peer with whom she shares something in common (e.g., similar interests). This pairing can be formal (such as assigning the two students to a partnership on a long-term project) or informal (such as encouraging the two to socialize), and can involve interaction in person or online. A tight friendship, particularly one with a student who can mentor the GC, can help an asynchronously developing GC more easily navigate her growth and differences.

- View the student as special/exceptional in the same way you would view a student with cognitive challenges as special/exceptional. This will help you avoid frustration when the GC acts out, and to successfully treat adverse behaviors with appropriate, methodical interventions.

- Guide the GC's emotional development just as you would guide students' cognitive development. For example, if a GC is overly pushy with peers, give the issue just as much attention and guidance as you would if he chronically failed to complete assignments.

- Garner outside-classroom support for GCs as needed. For example, if a GC's needs are not being met by the school's general education program, she can have an Individualized Education Program (IEP) (often erroneously thought to apply solely to students with cognitive disabilities). This added assistance can provide her with schoolwide staff support and help with behavior (via the development of a BIP), and the IEP can be especially important for twice-exceptional students.

Twice-Exceptional

Many gifted students are "2E" (twice-exceptional) in that they also have challenges that interfere with learning (e.g., dyslexia, autism, OCD, anxiety). "Research indicates the incidence of these students ranges from 2.5% to 36% of the gifted population" (Wormald & Vialle, 2011, p. v), even though schools often fail to formally identify 2E students and thus 2E numbers can seem lower (Wormald, Vialle, & Rogers, 2014). A wealth of sources land on or near the statistic of 17 percent of GCs being 2E (see Bade, 2015; Rogers, 2011; Silverman, 2013), whereas other (particularly older) sources tend to fall within the 2-percent to 7-percent range. Adequate identification plays a role in this number.

> Since most schools usually stop looking for exceptional abilities once a learning deficiency has been identified, [2Es'] giftedness will probably go unidentified. As many as 30 percent of gifted kids may have some form of learning disability, difference, or difficulty. (Winebrenner & Brulles, 2012, p. 24)

Due to the intellect of GCs, 2Es' challenges are often masked or undiscovered. Therefore, to detect each exceptionality, teachers must use more care in watching for signs they'd normally look for in non-GCs. The following list will help you navigate possible challenges that a GC may be experiencing. The items listed also relate to GCs who do not qualify as having a disability yet have difficulty relating to peers or have other social-emotional struggles.

- Learn 2E fundamentals. The National Association for Gifted Children (NAGC) offers a concise yet ample 2E guide—The Twice-Exceptional Dilemma—located at www.nagc.org/sites/default/files/key%20reports/twiceexceptional.pdf.
- Seek specialized guidance. 2E combinations are as unique in what they require from teachers as are the students who have them. For this reason, teachers should turn to studies, texts, and experts (such as district psychologists and special/exceptional education directors) for specialized guidance. Following is a sampling of such guidance for some common 2E characteristics.

  Dyslexia. Berninger and Abbott (2013) found that 19 percent of dyslexic students were superiorly gifted in verbal reasoning, and other GCs might never be discovered as dyslexic due to high intellect masking their struggles. Berninger and Abbott (2013) suggested that teachers of dyslexic GCs focus on the impaired working memory components within intellectually engaging lesson sets rather than only teach oral word reading and written spelling.

  ADHD. Fugate, Zentall, and Gentry (2013) found that gifted students with ADHD had poorer working memories, yet also had significantly greater creativity than non-ADHD GCs. While lessons appropriate for psychomotor OEs are obvious matches for many ADHD GCs, lessons appropriate for imaginational OEs are also likely to benefit many ADHD GCs.

Autism. Rubenstein et al. (2015) found that 2Es with Autism Spectrum Disorder had characteristics that are incompatible with typical educational environments, and school staff tended to disproportionately focus on students' strengths or weaknesses rather than showing consideration for both. Teachers can help autistic GCs by working closely with parents to find learning options suited to the GC's needs, and maintaining a balanced regard for both the student's strengths and weaknesses. For example, if the student is flourishing academically but refuses to interact with peers, the latter should not be ignored.

- Employ general 2E strategies. There are strategies that tend to work well with most 2Es, regardless of the combination of exceptionalities. Willard-Holt, Weber, Morrison, and Horgan (2013) found students with a range of exceptionalities rated certain teaching strategies as very beneficial.

Beneficial Strategy 1: Give students a sense of control over their own learning. Ninety-three percent of 2Es found it "very beneficial" (p. 253) to know, prior to assignment completion, how they would be graded, and 87 percent gave the same rating to knowing how much time they have to complete an assignment.

Beneficial Strategy 2: Empower students to think about complicated ideas in different ways. Eighty-six percent of 2Es found it "very beneficial" (p. 253) to understand ways ideas connect, how things happen, and why things happen, and 79 percent gave the same rating to understanding complex ideas and problems, and to dissecting big ideas and problems.

- Celebrate neurodiversity. That is, view different neurological characteristics as normal, valuable contributions to society. Activities in which there are roles likely to engage students with ADHD, roles likely to engage your students with autism, and so on can appeal to the range of 2Es, OEs, GCs, and non-GCs in your classroom.

Socioeconomically Disadvantaged

Even without a list declaring which of your students are socioeconomically disadvantaged (SD), you likely know who your poor kids are (e.g., students with worn out backpack or students without school supplies). Treading very carefully, and not using terms like "poor" as the reason behind your actions, you can serve as "match maker" between a parent of an SD GC and a parent you know to be very active in providing extracurricular opportunities to her child. For example, the SD GC could be invited to join the other family on some of their excursions. It's very important that you never reveal any student's personal details (like SD status) with other students or their parents.

Many extracurricular opportunities great for GCs are free (such as Imaginology [www.ocfair.com/steam/2016/index.php]). Share these opportunities with students and their parents, and encourage carpooling for students without rides.

English Learner (EL)

ELs who are also gifted are best served by the blending of programs: addressing and growing language skills while also involving the GC in activities that engage critical and creative thinking (Lewis, Rivera, & Roby, 2011). To hold off on gifted education until the EL is English proficient is damaging and unprincipled.

Personal Account: Most of my ELs spoke English better than they read or wrote English. My GC named Cho, however, was the reverse. She would have been redesignated as FEP long before I encountered her were it not for her poor English-speaking skills, compounded by severe shyness. I often paired her with the class' two other GCs, neither of whom spoke Cho's home language, to work on advanced content. I noticed Cho was being largely left out of the trio's discussions. I spoke with all three students about the need for Cho to speak as much as each of the other two, as her contributions were just as important. To ensure Cho was "being heard" (but also to work on Cho's ability to be understood), I asked these students to repeat what Cho was saying to them whenever they doubted they heard Cho correctly. This served as an exercise in listening for Cho's peers and gave them time to consider the added perspective Cho offered on the content with which they worked. It also let Cho hear her words said back in a way that was clear and error-free. Most importantly, it allowed Cho, who reached a point of sharing unabashedly in this supportive trio, to work in earnest on GC-appropriate content.

Underachievement

This book's other sections combat underachievement (such as by engaging GCs so they are motivated to live up to their potential). However, there are additional reasons GCs might struggle academically. For example, GCs might be disorganized (e.g., lose homework or miss due dates), procrastinate, turn in sloppy work, have poor handwriting, or hide their intellect in order to fit in with peers or appeal to a peer on whom they have a crush. Avoid jumping to conclusions (like assuming that the GC "doesn't care") if a GC underperforms.

Likewise, because a GC is gifted in one or more areas does not guarantee giftedness in all areas (Subotnik, Olszewski-Kubilius, & Worrell, 2011). Thus, a GC might need added support with some academics.

Work with the GC and parents to determine the heart of the problem so you can recommend and support a targeted course of action. Setting weekly goals with the GC and revisiting them throughout the week as needed can prove effective.

Final Thoughts

By choosing to read this book, you clearly understand that GCs have unique issues and needs and are just as worthy of teachers' consideration as non-GCs. By knowing who your GCs are, what their particular qualities are, and how you can challenge and engage them, you are well armed to meet the needs of all of your GCs in a single, diverse classroom. Thank you for your commitment to making school a rewarding place for these precious children.

ENCORE

HELPFUL RESOURCES

Using this book as a guide, complete the graphic organizer shown in Figure 4 for each of your GCs. Keeping these sheets handy as you plan lessons will help you craft appropriate opportunities for every GC to provide optimum engagement and challenge.

Check out resources, sign up for newsletters, and more at:

- Association for the Education of Gifted Underachieving Students (AEGUS)—www.aegus1.org.
- 2e Twice-Exceptional Newsletter—www.2enewsletter. com.
- Hoagies' Gifted Education Page—www.hoagiesgifted. org.
- Mensa for Kids—www.mensaforkids.org—which includes lesson on intensities—http://www. mensaforkids.org/teach/lesson-plans/intensities-in-the-classroom/.
- National Association for Gifted Children (NAGC)—www.nagc.org—which includes the National Standards in Gifted and Talented Education—http:// www.nagc.org/resources-publications/resources/ national-standards-gifted-and-talented-education.
- Potential Plus UK—www.potentialplusuk.org.
- Supporting Emotional Needs of the Gifted (SENG)—http://sengifted.org.

FIGURE 4: **Gifted Child Notes**

Complete this sheet for each gifted child (put his/her name in the center) and keep it private.

Overexcitabilities

The child's OEs are:

☐ Emotional
☐ Imaginational
☐ Intellectual
☐ Psychomotor
☐ Sensual

Notes to guide how I handle and leverage these OEs:

Hidden Challenges

The child has these challenges:

☐ Asynchronous development
☐ 2E: _____
☐ Socioeconomically
   disadvantaged
☐ English learner
☐ Other (e.g., underachiever):
   _____

Notes to guide how I help the child overcome or navigate these challenges:

Engagement

Consider the child's:

☐ Standard-Specific Level
☐ Interests
☐ Extroversion vs. introversion
☐ Learning preferences (multiple
   intelligences, learning modali-
   ties, etc.)
☐ Other preferences

Notes to guide my lesson choices and differentiation for this child:

Challenge

When needed, acceleration approaches that tend to work best for the child are:

☐ Speed up lesson
☐ Skip ahead on lesson
☐ Skip to higher grade/level
☐ Go more in depth
☐ Work on different content

Notes on which enrichment opportunities I will offer this child:

A downloadable version of this organizer is available at http://www.ascd.org/ASCD/pdf/books/rankin2016.pdf (or click on "Online Bonus Content" on the book's Table of Contents on the ASCD website—http://www.ascd.org/publications/books/sf117019.aspx).

References

Azzam, A. (2016). Six strategies for challenging gifted learners. *Education Update, 58*(4). Alexandra, VA: Association for Supervision and Curriculum Development.

Bade, J. M. (2015, May). 2e and IDEA: The right to assessment and services. *2e Newsletter*. Retrieved from http://www.2enewsletter.com/subscribers_only/arch_2015_5_2e%20and%20IDEA_JMB.html.

BBC. (2012). *US teen invents advanced cancer test using Google*. Retrieved from http://www.bbc.co.uk/news/magazine-19291258.

Berninger, V. W., & Abbott, R. D. (2013). Differences between children with dyslexia who are and are not gifted in verbal reasoning. *Gifted Child Quarterly, 57*(4), 223–233.

Callahan, C. M., Moon, T. R., & Oh, S. (2014). *National surveys of gifted programs executive summary*. Charlottesville, VA: National Research Center on the Gifted and Talented University of Virginia.

Card, D., & Giuliano, L. (2015). *Can universal screening increase the representation of low income and minority students in gifted education?* (Working Paper No. 21519). Cambridge, MA: National Bureau of Economic Research. Retrieved from www.nber.org/papers/w21519.

Colangelo, N., Assouline, S., & Gross, M. U. M. (2004). *A nation deceived: How schools hold back America's brightest students (Vol. 1)*. Iowa City, IA: University of Iowa, Connie Belin & Jacqueline N. Blank International Center for Gifted Education and Talent Development.

Colucci, A. (2015). Gifted ed. students are more than just really smart kids. *Education Week Teacher*. Retrieved from www.edweek.org/tm/articles/2015/11/24/understanding-gifted-students.html.

Dweck, C. S. (2008). *Mindset: The new psychology of success*. New York, NY: Random House.

Edutopia. (2013, August 13). How making robots captivates kids' imaginations. *Edutopia*. Retrieved from http://www.edutopia.org/is-school-enough-robotics-mentoring-video.

Fonseca, C. (2011). Emotional intensity in gifted students: Helping kids cope with explosive feelings. Waco, TX: Prufrock Press Inc.

Freeman, J. (2010). *Gifted lives: What happens when gifted children grow up*. New York, NY: Routledge.

Fugate, C. M., Zentall, S. S., & Gentry, M. (2013). Creativity and working memory in gifted students with and without characteristics of attention deficit hyperactive disorder lifting the mask. *Gifted Child Quarterly, 57*(4), 234–246.

Grissom, J. A., Redding, C. (2016). Discretion and disproportionality: Explaining the underrepresentation of high-achieving students of color in gifted programs. *AERA Open.* Retrieved from http://ero.sagepub.com/content/2/1/2332858415622175. Sage Journals, doi: 10.1177/2332858415622175.

Lewis, L. C., Rivera, A., Roby, D. (2011). *Identifying and serving culturally and linguistically diverse gifted students.* Waco, TX: Prufrock Press Inc.

Long, C. (2013). Are we failing gifted students? *neaToday.* Retrieved from http://neatoday.org/2013/09/18/are-we-failing-gifted-students-2.

National Association for Gifted Children. (2011). *Position statement: Redefining giftedness for a new century: Shifting the paradigm.* Retrieved from http://www.nagc.org/sites/default/files/Position%20Statement/Redefining%20Giftedness%20for%20a%20New%20Century.pdf.

National Association for Gifted Children (2016). *Gifted education in the U.S.* Retrieved from https://www.nagc.org/resources-publications/resources/gifted-education-us.

Renzulli, J. S., & Park, S. (2002). Giftedness and high school dropouts: Personal, family, and school-related factors (RM02168). Storrs: University of Connecticut, The National Research Center on the Gifted and Talented.

Rogers, K. (2002). *Re-forming gifted education: How parents and teachers can match the program to the child.* Scottsdale, AZ: Great Potential Press.

Rogers, K. B. (2011). Thinking smart about twice exceptional learners: steps for finding them and strategies for catering to them appropriately. In C. Wormald & W. Vialle (Eds.), *Dual Exceptionality*, (pp. 57–70). New South Wales, Australia: Australian Association for the Education of the Gifted and Talented LTD.

Rubenstein, L. D., Schelling, N., Wilczynski, S. M., Hooks, E. N. (2015). Lived experiences of parents of gifted students with Autism Spectrum Disorder: The struggle to find appropriate educational experiences. *Gifted Child Quarterly, 59*(4), 283–298.

Silverman, L. (2013). What we have learned about gifted children. *Gifted Development Center.* Retrieved from http://www.gifteddevelopment.com/articles/what-we-have-learned-about-gifted-children.

Stanley, T. (2012). *Project-based learning for gifted students: A handbook for the 21st-century classroom.* Waco, TX: Prufrock Press Inc.

Subotnik, R. F., Olszewski-Kubilius, P., & Worrell, F. C. (2011). Rethinking giftedness and gifted education: A proposed direction forward based on psychological science. *Psychological Science in the Public Interest, 12* (1), 3–54. doi: 10.1177/1529100611418056.

Whittenberg, S. (2015). Gifted gab: What is 2E? *Oracle, 44*(2). Arlington, TX: Mensa.

Willard-Holt, C., Weber, J., Morrison, K. L., & Horgan, J. (2013). Twice-exceptional learners' perspectives on effective learning strategies. *Gifted Child Quarterly, 57*(4), 247–262.

Winebrenner, S. (2001). *Teaching gifted kids in the regular classroom: Strategies and techniques every teacher can use to meet the academic needs of the gifted and talented.* Minneapolis, MN: Free Spirit Publishing.

Winebrenner, S., & Brulles, D. (2012). *Teaching gifted kids in today's classroom: Strategies and techniques every teacher can use.* Minneapolis, MN: Free Spirit Publishing.

Wormald, C., & Vialle, W. (2011). *Dual exceptionality.* New South Wales, Australia: Australian Association for the Education of the Gifted and Talented LTD.

Wormald, C., Vialle, W., & Rogers, K. (2014). Young and misunderstood in the education system: A case study of giftedness and specific learning disabilities. *Australasian Journal of Gifted Education, 23*(2), 16–28.

Related Resources

At the time of publication, the following ASCD resources were available (ASCD stock numbers appear in parentheses). For up-to-date information about ASCD resources, go to www.ascd.org. You can search the complete archives of *Educational Leadership* at http://www.ascd.org/el.

ASCD Edge Group
Exchange ideas and connect with other educators interested in inclusion on the social networking site ASCDEdge® at http://ascdedge.ascd.org/.

Print Products
Educational Leadership: Resilience & Learning (September 2013) (#114018)

Educational Leadership: For Each to Excel (February 2012) (#112020)

Align the Design: A Blueprint for School Improvement by Nancy J. Mooney and Ann T. Mausbach (#108005)

For more information, send e-mail to member@ascd.org; call 1-800-933-2723 or 703-578-9600, press 2; send a fax to 703-575-5400; or write to Information Services, ASCD, 1703 N. Beauregard St., Alexandria, VA 22311-1714 USA.

About the Author

Jenny Grant Rankin, PhD, teaches the Post Doc Masterclass at the University of Cambridge. Dr. Rankin, who resides in California most of the year, earned a PhD in Education, with a specialization in School Improvement Leadership. She is an award-winning former junior high school teacher who earned such honors as being named Teacher of the Year and having the American flag flown over the US Capitol building in honor of her dedication to her students. As the majority of her students were socio-economically disadvantaged English learners, she specialized in using data, differentiation, and creative instruction (e.g., gamification, project-based learning, global learning) to ensure that her exceptional students were being challenged and engaged even as they learned alongside struggling and grade-level learners. Dr. Rankin, a Mensan who grew up in GT/GATE/TAG, is the assistant coordinator of her county's Mensa Gifted Youth Program and the author of numerous books and journal articles.